All Kinds of Poems
for All Kinds of Kids

"If the mark of a great poem
is something you wish you'd written
then this collection is full of them."

— PAUL COOKSON

"David's work has appeared in just about
all of the 50 or so anthologies
that I've compiled …
an engaging performer
equally at home with both
serious and humorous poetry."

— BRIAN MOSES

"Quirky and quizzical,
David Harmer writes
wonderful poems
for all kinds of kids in all manner of moods,
and he really does know
how to find the rhymes."

— HARRIET TARLO

To John

ALL KINDS OF POEMS
FOR ALL KINDS OF KIDS

David Harmer

Illustrated by Ted Schofield

Love
Dav

[look what you started!!!]

SMALL | DONKEY

the poetry business

Published 2021 by Smith|Donkey
an imprint of The Poetry Business
Campo House,
54 Campo Lane,
Sheffield S1 2EG
www.poetrybusiness.co.uk

Copyright © Poems by David Harmer 2021
Copyright © Illustrations by Ted Schofield 2021
The moral rights of the author have been asserted.
ISBN 978-1-912196-39-5

All rights reserved.
Without limiting the rights under copyright reserved above,
no part of this publication may be reproduced, storied in or introduced
into a retrieval system, or transmitted, in any form or by any means
(electronic, mechanical, photocopying, recording or otherwise),
without the prior written permission of both the copyright owner
and the above publisher of this book.

Designed & typeset by The Poetry Business.
Printed by CPI.

British Library Cataloguing-in-Publication Data.
A catalogue record for this book is available from the British Library.

The Poetry Business is a member of Inpress
www.inpressbooks.co.uk.
Distributed by NBN International, 1 Deltic Avenue,
Rooksley, Milton Keynes MK13 8LD.

The Poetry Business gratefully acknowledges the support
of Arts Council England.

FOR EUAN AND JUDE

CONTENTS

13	ALL KINDS OF KIDS
16	GRANDPA'S STORIES
18	WH—O—O—O—O—P—S!!!
20	PASS IT ON IT'S REALLY TRUE!
22	PASTING PATSY'S PASTY POSTERS
23	MY MUM PUT ME ON THE TRANSFER LIST
24	GREAT-GREAT GRANDAD BEN
26	DAYTIME MOON
27	A GOODNIGHT MOON
28	AUTUMN MOON
29	SLICK NICK'S DOG'S TRICKS
30	A POEM THAT THINKS IT'S
32	THE HISTORY OF NOTHING
34	WHISPERS OUTSIDE THE GRAVEYARD
36	THE VISITOR
38	DON'T MUCK ABOUT WITH GIANTS
42	HARRY HOBGOBLIN'S SUPERSTORE
44	WHEN THE GROWN-UPS ARGUE

47	TWELVE LINES THAT ARE ALL ABOUT ME, NOT YOU, JUST ME, SO THERE, NER-NER.
48	THE PIRATES' SHANTY
50	SOME SILLIES
52	LEARNING IN LOCKDOWN
54	LOCKDOWN DAD
56	MY THIN BROTHER
58	WHAT EUAN TOLD HIS LITTLE BROTHER JUDE ON DECEMBER 18TH
59	ALWAYS LISTEN TO YOUR MATES
61	HEAD OVER HEELS
62	PLAYING TENNIS WITH JUSTIN
64	MILLIE'S MIRROR POEM
66	OUR TREE
68	ONE MOMENT IN SUMMER
70	DIY ASTRONAUT
72	THREE HAPPY BIRTHDAYS ON FARAWAY PLANETS
73	THE WORST PLACE TO FIND AN ALIEN
76	A VERY TIRED POEM

INTRODUCTION

I was a lucky boy because I grew up in a house full of books and poetry with grown-ups who read to me. I started reading and writing poems and stories then and I haven't stopped. I remember when I was about nine, I learned 'The Walrus and the Carpenter' and 'Jabberwocky' (by Lewis Carrol) and performed them to the class. I chose those two because they were funny, using fantastic words and telling strange stories. I was always a bit of a show-off and I still love reading poems to people.

There were very few poems for children around in The Olden Days, but now there are loads of wonderful poetry books to enjoy. I think poems are clever lists that turn ordinary things into magical things, so if I look at a school yard I might think, 'What if a space ship full of slimy aliens landed here right now? What if my table came to life as a huge monster? Is my best mate really a robot?' Then I decide what kind of poem I need to write to tell that story. Sometimes poems ask serious questions, sometimes they just rock and roll along with loads of rhymes and bounce. Others are twisty and tiny, some don't rhyme at all and some make different shapes. I love them all.

When I'm asked for tips on becoming a writer what I always say is this: read a lot of books and write a lot of poems. Then, read them to your friends and to the grown-ups too. Have fun doing it! Poems are there to make your words dance and sing, to make them thoughtful, to make them change the world around you. Make some of your own, stand up and shout them out as loudly as you can!

David Harmer
May 2021

ALL KINDS OF KIDS

The batty and the chatty
The scatty and the catty
The dippy and the lippy
The gobby and the snobby
The loopy and the droopy
The soppy and the floppy
The feared and revered
The one with a beard!

The ones who run in races
The ones who pull daft faces
The smiley and the wily
The pretty and the gritty
The ones who jump about
The ones who like to shout
The squirmers and the squigglers
The weirdos and the gigglers.

The braggers and the boasters
The clever make-the-mosters
The surly and the twirly
The girlie and the burly
The ones who chew their nails
The ones who tell big tales
The ones who save their dosh
The ones who talk dead posh

The fizzy and the dizzy
The bossy and the busy

The snidey and the snooty
The ones who are a beauty
The cool and the cooler
The fooled and the fooler
The posers and the liars
The bust-a-gut-triers.

The grotty and the snotty
The nerdy and the wordy
The dreamy and the screamy
The ones who make you weary
The ones who talk like crazy
The ones who are quite lazy
The ones we all adore
The ones who are a bore.

The wary and the scary
The freaky and the geeky
The cheery and the sneery
The stinky and the slinky
The spotty and the dotty
The lumpy and the grumpy
The ones who like to natter
The ones with chat-up patter.

All kinds of kids
Every one unique
Every one matters
Every day and every week
Got to help each other
Got to pull through
Don't care if you don't like it
It's what you've got to do.

GRANDPA'S STORIES

Grandpa says he's so old
that when he was seven
he lived next door to Queen Victoria.
They took the dinosaurs
for a walk in the park every morning.
Being quite small
Her Majesty had a lot of trouble
with the Tyrannosaurus Rex.

Grandpa says yesterday
a pirate ship sailed on the lake in the park,
a skull and crossbones flying from the mast.
All the bloodthirsty crew
swarmed up the rigging, jumped
with pistols and cutlasses
into the playground, swung on the swings,
dug up the football pitch for treasure
and marooned the first mate
on the traffic island across the road.

Grandpa says he knows for certain
that a spaceship the size of a wheelie-bin
landed on our school field last Thursday –
slimy aliens like giant slugs
slid through a crack in the wall.
They searched the whole building for us kids
wanting to suck out our brains.

'But I'm not sure if you lot
have got any brains,' laughed Grandpa.
I really like listening to my Grandpa,
and all his stories are true.

WH—O—O—O—O—P—S!!!

      Yesterday

I   picked
                      up   the
most
beautiful

     G L A S S
G   L   A   S   S
                        glass
                        glass
g l a s s SNOWGLOBE

     you   have   take care
               ever   take care
    seen

BUT **SUDDENLY** I   tripped
                 over
                     because I
was
       wearing slippy sloppy socks

and   I-I-I-I   **D**   smash
              R   crash
              O
              P
              P
              E
              D
              it

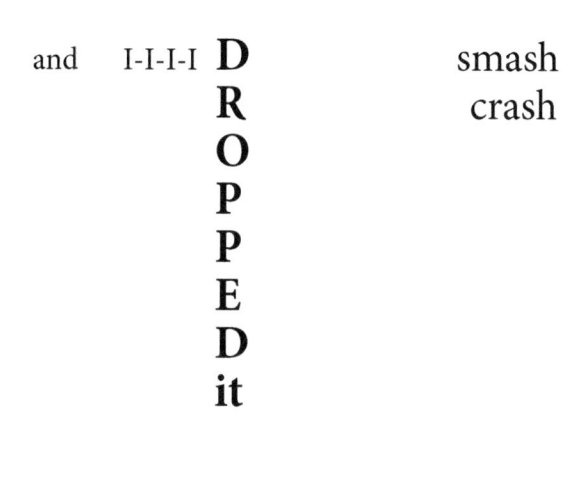

Oh no no   no no

MY BEAUTIFUL S   sm
          N O W G   i
                   L O B E   ther
         smashed   to
    eeeeeeeeeeeens

   on the tiled floor of the kitchen and our
dog Bertie ate the snowman's nose.

PASS IT ON IT'S REALLY TRUE!

Our headmaster Mr. Pugh
Kissed our teacher, sweet Miss Drew
Hannah had a perfect view
From outside the Y6 loo
Clare and Rachel saw it too
They told me, now I've told you
Pass it on, it's really true.

Hey guess what? No-one knew
Our crazy cook makes lunchtime stew
With doo-doos from a kangaroo
She bought quite cheaply at the zoo
Then mixes treacle tart with glue
Jack and Billy heard it too
Pass it on, it's really true.

Did you know that it was James
Wrote on the school wall during games?
With a pen he pinched from Sky
She got told off, which made her cry,
And Dev loves Jade and she loves Paul
Paul loves Song who loves them all.
Pass it on, it's really true.

Kyle put paint in Kieran's shoe
When he was in the dinner queue
Kieran didn't have a clue

Why his socks had turned bright blue
But thanks to me he soon knew –
You see I told him it was you!
Pass it on, it's really true.

*Pass it on, pass it on, pass it on
It's really true.*

PASTING PATSY'S PASTY POSTERS

Petra Porter pastes in precincts
Patsy's pasty pasties poster
Patsy's posters for her pasties
And her tasty pasty pasta.

Patsy pays a pretty penny
For Petra's posters in the precincts
But Paula pastes her posters faster
Passes Petra, pasting past her.

So Patsy's pasting Paula's posters
Paying pasty Paula plenty
For faster pasta poster pasting
Pasting pasta posters faster.

MY MUM'S PUT ME ON THE TRANSFER LIST

On Offer:
One nippy striker, ten years old
Has scored seven goals this season
Has nifty footwork and a big smile
Knows how to dive in the penalty box
Can get filthy and muddy within two minutes
Guaranteed to wreck his kit each week
This is a FREE TRANSFER
But he comes with running expenses
Weeks of washing shirts and shorts
Socks and vests, a pair of trainers
Needs to eat huge amounts
Of chips and burgers, beans and apples
Water, Coke, crisps and oranges
Endless packets of chewing gum.
This offer open until the end of the season
I'll have him back then
At least until the cricket starts.
Any takers?

GREAT-GREAT GRANDAD BEN

I found this battered photo
Shoved inside a drawer
Looked inside a soldier's eyes
And this is what I saw.

A thousand fields of poppies
That bloomed as red as blood
And weary lines of soldiers
Trudging through the mud.

I heard the guns and shellfire
The cries of wounded men
The smoke and heat of battle
Round Great-Great Grandad Ben.

In the thick of warfare
With so many others
Fighting for our freedom
With his band of brothers.

How many pals did he lose
Through those dreadful years?
How many times did his face
Crumple with fresh tears?

November 1918
It all stopped for Ben
Silenced guns, peace declared
So he marched home again.

Bess his wife and Fred their son
Waited at the door
To welcome back a hero
From four long years of war.

He's here, my Great-Great Grandad,
Looking cool and calm
With his best mate beside him
Standing arm in arm.

It was all so long ago
The light of Time's so dim,
His picture's always on my wall
So I remember him.

DAYTIME MOON

Today we were driving home
from seeing our Grandpa
and Grandma on the other
side of town and it was still
bright daylight, even though
it was late, almost bedtime
and I looked out of the car
and suddenly saw
a small, pale moon
staring down at me
through silver clouds
and where the jet planes
had scratched deep smoky
plumes through the blue.
I turned to tell my mum
but she was falling asleep,
my dad was busy driving
and telling my little sister
to stop going on about
princesses and unicorns,
not to mention pink ponies
and all that rubbish, his
words not mine, so finally
it was just me and the moon
looking at each other.
I poked Mum quite hard
but by the time she'd
finished saying WHAT?
the shiny moon
had gone.

A GOODNIGHT MOON

A thin silver needle
stitches the moon to the sky

like a pearl button
reflecting

dark blue clouds
with bright edges.

It's like a quiet sea
calmed, barely breathing.

Time for my curtains to close
whisper goodnight.

AUTUMN MOON

This afternoon,
the moon blinked
its cold stone eye
for a minute or two,

then slid
behind thick clouds
swirling like fog
over the sea.

Yesterday it peeped
through a crack in the sky,
like an old man
at a window

tugging ragged curtains
for a long, sly look.
His smile split
in a yellow curve.

Tonight I know
the light will be silver,
streaming down
through diamond stars

bright as flames,
our shadows will shiver
on quiet streets
the colour of moondust.

SLICK NICK'S DOG'S TRICKS

Slick Nick's dog does tricks
The tricks Nick's dog does are slick
He picks up sticks, stands on bricks
Nick's finger clicks, the dog barks *SIX*!
He picks a mix of doggy bix
Then gives Slick Nick thick sloppy licks.
Mick and Rick's dog's not so quick
Kicks the bricks, drops the sticks
Can't bark to six, is in a fix
Gets Mick and Rick to do its tricks
Gets on their wicks despite its mix
Of waggy tail and loving licks.
But Slick Nick's dog does tricks
The tricks Nick's dog does are slick.

A POEM THAT THINKS IT'S

```
                grass  hop
                              per
    a
```

OR
PERHAPS   g
            r
    a   f   o

OR
SOME i n d of   s   bird
      k   w   g
                      o   n
                        o   i
                         p

OR   slidey   sl   ery
EVEN a sssslippy   ith   slimline slender
                erpent
  slappy sidewinder s   ine snake

OR
MAYBE a   verysmall
            veryquiet
            whiskery
            whispery
            mouse

                            d
                        o
OR
JUST   c
     a big cro   eating a GIGANTIC
            i
             l
                    e
                            SAND
                        slug and cheese
                            WICH

                                Yummy
OR
SIMPLY
         somewordsstucktogetherlikethisinordertomakealine
         or two
         or even three.
IS
VERY *difficult to read.*

31

THE HISTORY OF NOTHING

'Once there was nothing,
then a pebble of gas and dust,
rock and atoms plus swirling,
fantastic energies all exploded
in a Big Bang!' said our teacher.

'My brain hurts,' whispered Sanjay.

'It made the universe,
which stretched and expanded,
growing bigger and bigger, creating
stars and suns, moons and planets,
like our planet Earth,' said our teacher.

'And dinosaurs?' asked Sanjay.

'Yes and humans later on
and oxygen, carbon dioxide, oceans,
clouds, skies and it didn't stop. It's still spinning
outwards, making Black Holes, new nebulae
and galaxies,' said our teacher.

'And aliens?' laughed Sanjay.

'Don't know about that
Sanjay but thank you for asking.
And there was nothing at all there before
this explosion, just empty darkness
going on forever,' said our teacher.

'What's nothing?' asked Sanjay.

'Ten minus ten,' smiled Chloe.
'But there must have been something
you can't just have nothing. Nothing is a Something
if that's all there is,' said Sanjay.
'Well there was nothing,' said our teacher.

'Now is that the bell?'

'I think they make this stuff up
to confuse us, even if it's true,' I said
on the yard but Sanjay wasn't listening,
he was playing football with Smigsy
so I went in goal

and we won five-nothing.

WHISPERS OUTSIDE THE GRAVEYARD

Where are we going? *Into the graveyard.*

Why are we going? *Wait and see.*

When are we going? *Round about midnight.*

Who will be going? *Just you and me.*

Who will I see there? *Skeletons playing.*

Why are we going? *For some fun.*

What if I don't want to? *Well, you have to.*

What's that moaning? *The fun has begun!*

What if it's scary? *Well, it will be.*

Very very scary? *Yes, that's right.*

Really scary skeletons? *At least two hundred.*

When will I come home? *Not tonight.*

Not tonight? *That's right*
No-one at all
Goes home tonight!

THE VISITOR

It was late last night I'm certain
that I saw my bedroom curtain
twitch and flutter
felt a chill, heard him mutter
'Hullo lad I'm back.'

Uncle Jack!
Dead since this time last year.
A pickled onion in his beer
stopped his breath
a sudden death
that sadly took us by surprise.

But there he was, those eyes
one grey, one blue
one through
which the light could pass
the other, glass.

He drifted down, swam about
In his brown suit, flat cap, stout
boots and tie.
I saw him take out his eye.

'It's not a dream
this,' he said, 'don't scream
I'll not come back, I shan't return.'
Then I felt the ice-cold burn
of his glass eye upon my skin.

Saw his ghastly, ghostly grin.
'Don't worry, don't get in a stew
just thought I'd keep an eye on you.'

When I woke up today
I saw the blue eye, not the grey
but when I picked it up to go
it drained away like melting snow.
Didn't it?

DON'T MUCK ABOUT WITH GIANTS

I can hear the heavy beat
Of his footsteps far away
I can feel the earthquake shaking
As he stomps my way today.

> *Thump-thump-thumperty thump!*
> *Thump-thump-thumperty thump!*

I can hear his groans and grunts
As he marches down the hill
I can hear his grumpy grumble
Getting clearer, nearer still.

> *Thump-thump-thumperty thump!*
> *Thump-thump-thumperty thump!*

I can see his big brown boots
His revolting hairy knees
He is almost here upon me
Taller than the tallest trees.

> *Thump-thump-thumperty thump!*
> *Thump-thump-thumperty thump!*

I can smell his stinky socks
And his foul, disgusting breath
I can hear his chomping teeth
He will frighten me to death!

> *Thump-thump-thumperty thump!*
> *Thump-thump-thumperty thump!*

Now I think I'm going to scream
Sick with fear and terrified
He's so hungry he will eat me
Mashed or boiled or fried.

> *Thump-thump-thumperty thump!*
> *Thump-thump-thumperty thump!*

Watch me hide behind this tree
He's not seen me after all
Look he's walking round the corner
Disappeared behind that wall.

Thump-thump-thumperty thump!
Thump-thump-thumperty thump!

Yes I think he's really gone
And at last I'm safe and free
I'll celebrate straight away
Big Fat Giant, can't catch me.

He heard me calling names
See, he's turning round to stare
Hear him growl and gnash his teeth
Yikes he's back! Just over there!

Thump-thump-thumperty
        thump!
Thump-thump-thumperty
        thump!

Time to run now for your life
Don't mess with giants, they're not nice
They grind your bones into powder
Just get lost, that's my advice.

Thump-thump-thumperty
        thump!
Thump-thump-thumperty
        thump!

CRUNCH!

HARRY HOBGOBLIN'S SUPERSTORE

You want a gryphon's feather
Or a spell to change the weather?
A pixilating potion
That helps you fly an ocean?
Some special brew of magic
To supercharge your broomstick?
Witches, wizards, why not pop
Into Harry's one-stop shop?

Tins of powdered dragons' teeth
Bottled beetles, newts.
Freeze-dried cobwebs, cats and rats
Screaming mandrake roots.
Lizard skins stirred widdershins
A giant's big toe-nail.
Secondhand spells used only once
New ones that can't fail.
Spells to grow some donkey's ears
On the teacher no-one likes
Spells to make you good at sums
Spells to find lost bikes.

Spells that grow
And stretch and shrink
Spells that make
Your best friends stink.
Sacks of spells
Stacked on my shelves

Come on in, see for yourselves.
Magic prices, bargains galore
At Harry Hobgoblin's Superstore.

WHEN THE GROWN-UPS ARGUE

Once again, what a pain
Dad's football team is losing

Defence is slack, no full back
The goalkeeper was snoozing.

On the couch, Dad's a grouch
His television viewing

In a word is disturbed
By what his team is doing.

He gives a shout, stomps about
Which makes Mum very cross.

I'll stop this row right now
Show them who is boss.

Mum and Dad listen up
Cease this dreadful noise.
Just sit there on the naughty step
Like all bad girls and boys.

Told you once, told you twice
Behaviour must improve.
You both sit still and have a think
Before I let you move.

They've settled down, no frown,
Stopped their silly fighting.

I'll make them see, they'll agree.
I'll get it down in writing.

Yes they're smiling, good-timing
Their gloomy moods are missing.

Wait, that's bad, really sad
Mum and Dad are kissing!

YUK YUK! Good luck
I'm out of the door.

Leave them to it, I blew it,
Just can't stand this any more!

TWELVE LINES THAT ARE ALL ABOUT ME, NOT YOU, JUST ME, SO THERE, NER-NER.

Some days
         like Sundays
I like to laze about.

Other days like Saturdays
         I like to yell and shout.

Mondays to Fridays
         I run through my school gates.

Fair enough
         I learn some stuff

BUT most of all
         I play football

With all my bezzie mates.

THE PIRATES' SHANTY

Yo Ho Ho, Yo Ho Ho
We are pirates, off we go!

Pirate Pete, Pirate Pete
Great big cutlass, smelly feet.

Pirate Mason, Pirate Mason
He has got his ugly face on.

Pirate Mick, Pirate Mick
Feeling really, really sick.

Pirate Luke, Pirate Luke
He's so sick he's going to ....
(Be very poorly over the side of the ship.)

Yo Ho Ho, Yo Ho Ho
We are pirates, off we go!

Pirate Mary, Pirate Mary
Really horrid, really scary!

Pirate Rose, Pirate Rose
Has a hook to pick her nose.

Pirate Hannah, Pirate Hannah
Got a really cool bandana.

Pirate Jane, Pirate Jane
Makes you walk the plank again.

Now I'm the Captain of this crew
And pirating is what we do
We sail across the salty waves
A ghastly group of nasty knaves.
We're not pleasant, we're not nice
Pinch your treasure in a trice
Shouting, singing Yo Ho Ho
We are pirates, off we go!

Pirate Jim, Pirate Jim
A shark has just eaten him.

Pirate Maisie, Pirate Maisie
Just watch out, she's going crazy.

Pirate Josh, Pirate Josh
Falling from the rigging SPLOSH!

Yo Ho Ho, Yo Ho Ho
We are pirates, off we go!

SOME SILLIES

I
asked
this poem
if it was
made with
eight lines
it replied
in German
Nein

I
asked
this poem
if it wanted

to look like
a   win
dow   frame

it replied
what a pane.

I
asked
this poem
if it
was funny

it replied
ha ha ha ha ha ha ha ha
ha ha ha ha ha ha ha ha
ha ha ha ha ha ha ha no

I
asked
this poem
if it
was fed
up of
me as
king all
these silly
quest
ions
and should I
be paying it
a lot of money
to be giving
me the
answers
it replied

YEEEEEEESSSSSSSS$$$$

LEARNING IN LOCKDOWN

Weeks ago, we did a lot of sums
as well as reading, writing,
drawing, colouring in.

We spent hours on what
Dad called 'Proper Exercise.'
Like running on the spot and star jumps.

So boring but he seemed pleased
and there were always some sweets
as a reward. Yummy.

It isn't like that now, we play
lots of computer games and don't
do many sums, or get many sweets.

But when Mum FaceTimes
Auntie Jane, we get loads of them
and work like mad on camera.

Or Auntie Jane goes on and on
about 'Those kids get away with murder
they'll grow up knowing nothing.'

Well, we know loads of stuff.
Mainly about grown-ups and
their promises of sweets.

One day our teachers will ask us
what did we learn in Lockdown?
We can tell them this much.

When it comes to sweets
and telling the truth to each other
Never Trust a Grown-Up!

LOCKDOWN DAD

It turns out that my Dad
isn't as good at maths
as he thinks.

We have a go every morning
after jumping up and down
to PE on the telly.

Dad is very good
at jumping up in the air,
not so good at landing.

Yesterday he almost
smashed the coffee table
when he dropped headfirst

onto the sofa and bounced,
for some reason he didn't think
it was nearly as funny as I did.

Then we tried outdoor
exercise on our bikes, Dad
couldn't get his helmet on.

'It's my lockdown rockstar hair-do,'
he said. When Mum had stopped
laughing at that one

she said 'Don't go out
in all that Lycra, you look like
a badly stuffed teddy bear.'

Now, back to all the sums
he can't do, especially
division. 'What's chunking

and what's it got to do
with bus stops?' He asked.
'You need gerzinters my lad.'

I looked blank, he sighed.
'What do they teach you
these days? You know

five goes into twenty-five
five times. Gerzinters.'
'That's not how Mr Wirth

taught us,' I replied, 'he does
it different.' 'Well he's wrong,'
said Dad. I looked at him.

'Mr Wirth is never wrong but
he's never going to be any good
at being my Dad,' I said.

MY THIN BROTHER

My
broth
er
Ernie
is
one of
the thin
nest
kids
you
will
ever
meet
skinny
ams
legs like
string
knees
like cricket
balls
and
feet
that seem
TOO BIG FOR
HIS LEGS.

But
I still
think
he's
the best
brother
a kid
ever
had
especially
when
it
comes
to peering
over
next
door's
fence
to see
where
our
football
has
landed
and
getting
it
back.

WHAT EUAN TOLD HIS LITTLE BROTHER JUDE ON DECEMBER 18TH

Seven sleeps 'til Santa
He's almost on his way,
Right now he's telling all his elves
To load his magic sleigh.

Seven sleeps 'til Santa
Until that special night,
He's feeding up his reindeer
For their fantastic flight.

Close your eyes now little dude
Beneath that silver moon,
Tonight's a night for sleeping Jude
He'll be here very soon.

Seven sleeps 'til Santa
Seven more to go
Until he flies through starry skies
In rain and frost and snow.

Seven sleeps 'til Santa
Yes Santa's nearly due
And he'll be here on Christmas Eve
With prezzies for us two.

When he's been I'll wake you up
A special morning like no other,
We'll open up our gifts together
Me and my little brother.

ALWAYS LISTEN TO YOUR MATES

Walking past the spooky house
Ghostly house, haunted house
DON'T GO IN!

Pushing through the crowded trees
Overgrown, spiky trees
DON'T GO IN!

Peering through broken windows
Cobwebbed, dusty windows
DON'T GO IN!

Knocking on the cracked front door
Creaking, crazy door
DON'T GO IN!

Climb the stairs to the top
There's a door at the top
DON'T GO IN!

Light shines beneath the door
Something groans behind the door
DON'T GO IN!

An upstairs window frames your face
Your HELP ME, screaming face
BUT WE'RE NOT GOING IN!

all over the hall floor.
was being sick
Spider Webb who
than me and also at
or done it better
had either fallen over
in my class who
smiling at all the others
stood upright
very carefully
and slowly, very, very
back to earth
my feet, got
I dropped to
round and round.
whirling, spinning
to feel dizzy, everything
I began
in a stupid O.
and closing
its mouth opening
like a goldfish in a bowl
swam about in my head
I was thinking
so all the thoughts
flooded my brain
that all the blood
I soon discovered
like a drooping flag.
flapping about

bent at the knee
or a broom handle, the other
like the mast of a ship
one leg stuck into the air
to stand on my head
I learned how
Yesterday at school

HEAD OVER HEELS

PLAYING TENNIS WITH JUSTIN

It's dinnertime and very sunny.
I'm in the yard playing tennis with Justin.
Justin is winning fifty-five nil.

He's got a proper tennis bat called a rocket.
I haven't got a rocket so he gave me his spare.
His rocket is filled up with string, mine isn't
Mine's got lots of holes.

If I hit the ball with the bit with no holes
It goes quite a long way, but usually
Justin says I've hit the net.

We haven't got a net but Justin says
He knows where the net would be
If we did have one.
Justin is very clever like that.

He's just scored fifteen more points
I nearly scored one a moment ago
But Justin said it was offside.
So the score is seventy-nil to him.

Justin says my score is called love
Not nil, well I don't love it much.
I keep losing, Justin says not to worry
I might score a six in a minute.

He says it's his second serve for juice.
Well, the dinner lady hasn't called our group
In yet, so I haven't had one serving or any juice.
I'm starving and it's very hot.

Justin says he's scored three more goals
And that I should keep my eye on the ball
Then I might hit it with my rocket.

If Justin doesn't shut up really quickly
I might hit him with my rocket.
I think tennis is rubbish.

Justin says we can play at cricket if I want
But I've got to go in goals.
Sometimes you just can't win
With Justin.

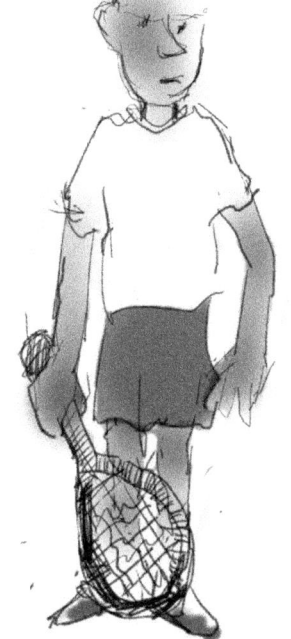

MILLIE'S MIRROR POEM

This
morning
I looked
into my
bedroom
mirror
and saw
not me in my
school uniform
but a caped
and masked
Super Hero
OK maybe not
just the usual
white polo shirt
grey skirt
red jumper
I know
it isn't going
to happen but
one day
it might.

This
morning
I looked
into my
bedroom
mirror
and saw
not me in my
school uniform
but a yellow and red caped
gold and silver masked
Super Millie flies through the skies
sorting out those Bad Guys
see the fear rise in their eyes
as I tear off their disguise
stop them telling all their lies
I Save The Day, no surprise
I know
it isn't going
to happen but
one day
it will.

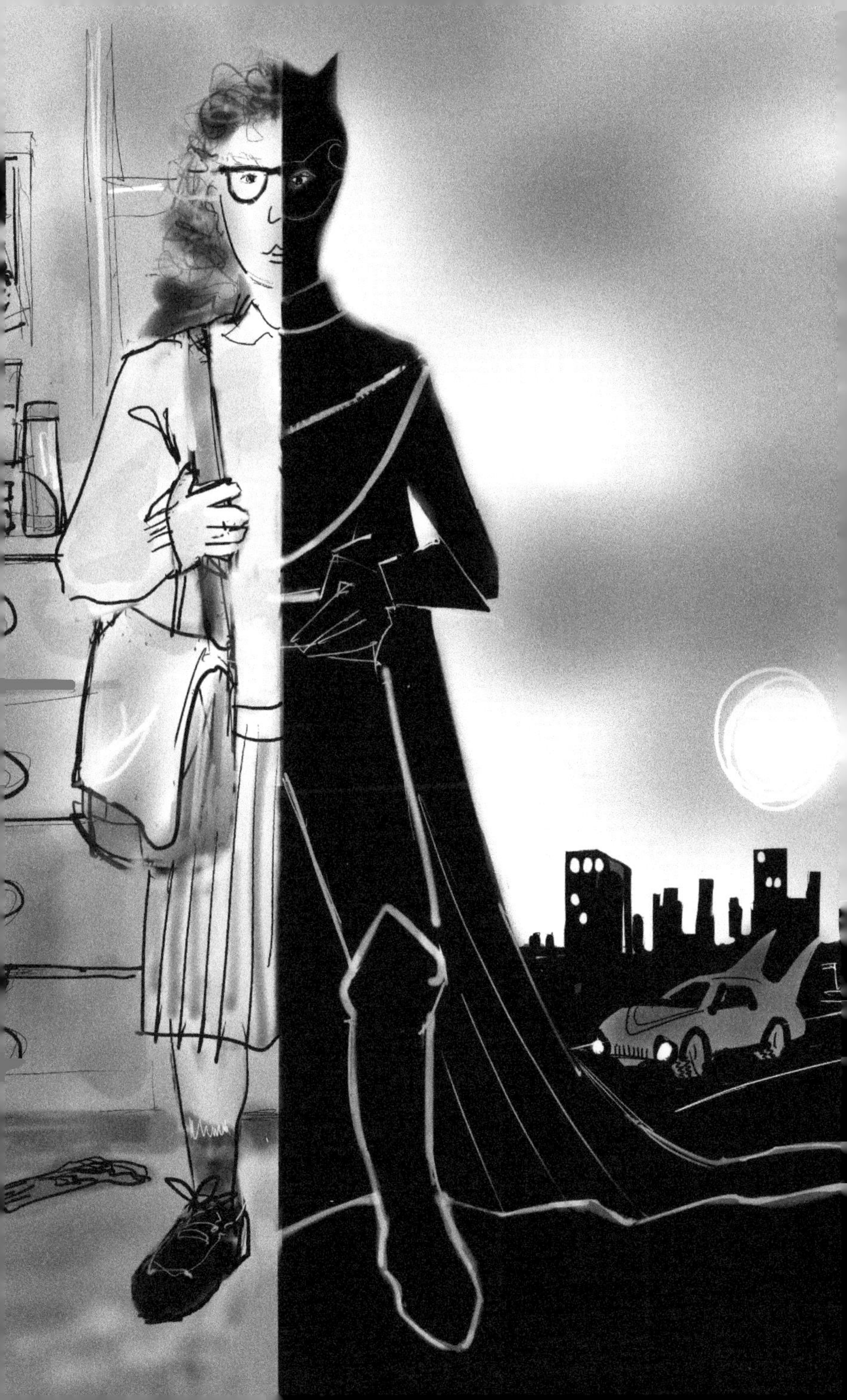

OUR TREE

It takes so long for a tree to grow
So many years of pushing the sky.

Long branches stretch their arms
Reach out with their wooden fingers.

Years drift by, fall like leaves
From green to yellow then back to green.

Since my grandad was a boy
And then before his father's father

There's been an elm outside our school
Its shadow long across our playground.

Today three men ripped it down
Chopped it up. It took ten minutes.

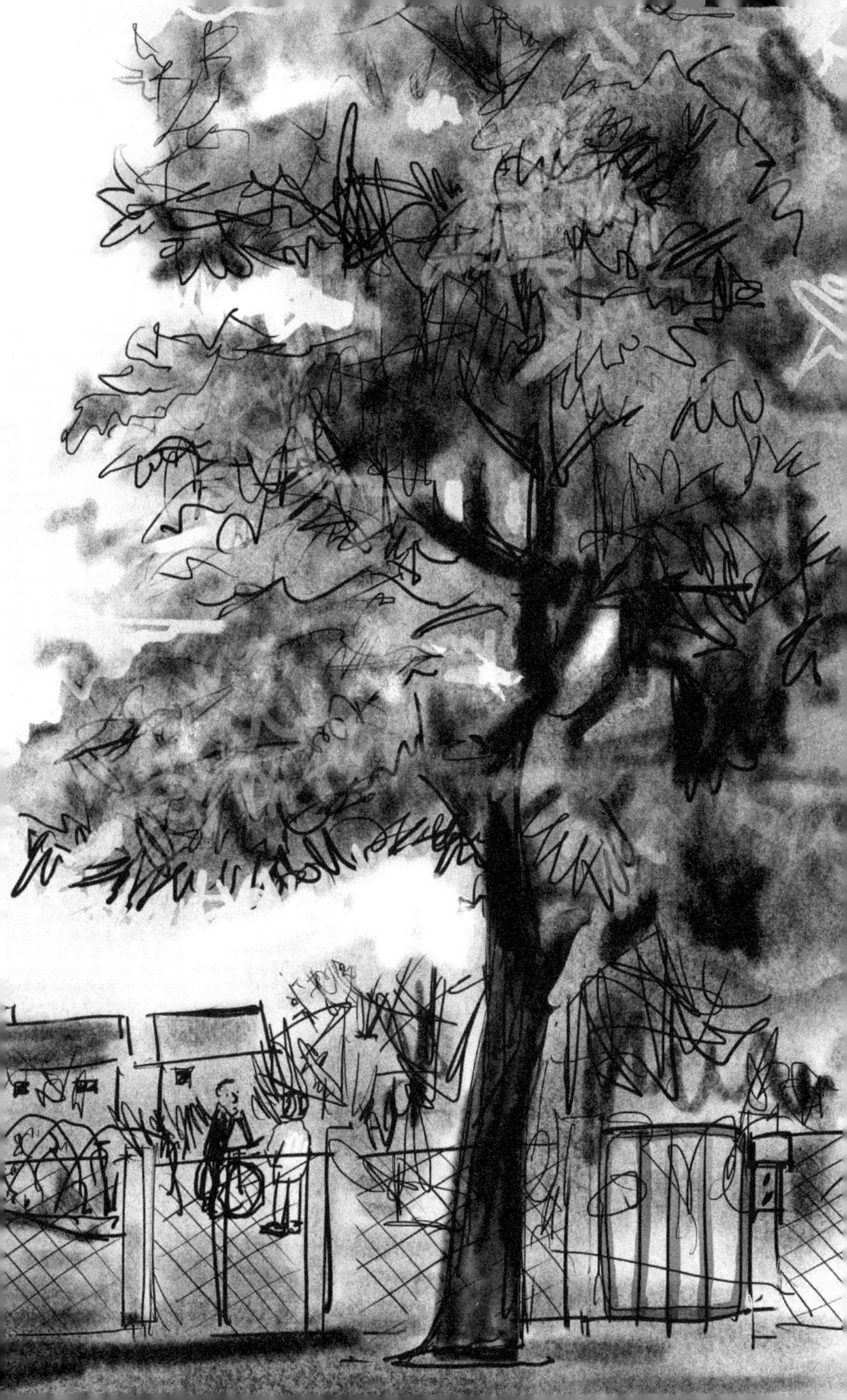

ONE MOMENT IN SUMMER

The house is dropping swallows
One by one from the gutter.

They swoop and fall
On our heads as we queue
For ice-cream.

It is so hot
That the long line of cars clogging the road
Shine and shimmer, stink of oil
The children gaze out from their misted windows.

The cars crawl round the curve
Of the road, stuck in between the shop
And the café.

My ice-cream is butterscotch and almond
Lizzie's is chocolate, Harriet's vanilla.

They are so delicious and cold
We lick them slowly, letting the long, cool flavours
Slide down our tongues.

Inside the cars, the red-faced people
Begin to boil.

The swallows flit and dart
Specks of blueblack and white
The summer flies at us
Like an arrow.

DIY ASTRONAUT

Dad's so good at DIY
He's decided he can fly
What a laugh, who'd have thought
The DIY astronaut.

Last night he shouted 'All those stars!
With bits and pieces from some cars
An oily lorry's cogs and wheels
Squirms from worms and leaping eels
The wings off some old aeroplane
Sizzling thoughts inside my brain
Bags of nails from The Sales
The singing of a thousand whales
Some magic beans, giant stalks
The fizz and pop of champagne corks
A hammer, a spanner, a socket set
Lumps of coal, a passing jet
Ten springs, a ladder and the roar
Of Billy's motorbike next door
Two tins of Special Elbow Grease
Permission from the Space Police
The whoop and glee of lambs in spring
The buoyant hope that joy can bring
The energy from ten tall rockets
Rubber bands in my pockets
A bungee rope, a catapult
A wild, frenetic somersault
A really bouncy trampoline

The biggest bubble you've ever seen
The steaming hiss from twenty kettles
The leap you get when you sit on nettles.
Mix them up with great care
And I could get myself up there!'

Dad's so good at DIY
He's decided he can fly
What a laugh, who'd have thought
The DIY astronaut.

THREE HAPPY BIRTHDAYS ON FARAWAY PLANETS

1

Hairy nostrils to you
Hairy nostrils to you
Hairy nostrils dear Fur Covered Alien Monster From Apeworld
Hairy nostrils to you.

2

Helpy Biffydoodle to yoggle
Holpy Boffydiddle to yurgle
Halpy Dobbleboffle dear Swaddlecotburger
Helpy Snoddybother to yiggle.

3

Beep Beep Beep   Beepbeep
Beep Beep Beep   Beepbeep
Beep Beep dear 14790345ZSP Robot Waste Disposal Unit Second Class
Beep Beep Beep   Beepbeep.

THE WORST PLACE TO FIND AN ALIEN

Don't know how it got there
Just know that it's true
The day that I discovered
The alien down the loo.

I shouted for my dad
Not knowing what to do
He arrived and said 'What's that
The alien down the loo?'

He stuck his head right down there
To get a better view
Saw a purple, splodgy thing
The alien down the loo.

It had long scaly legs
Nipping crab claws too
Nobody could sit upon
The alien down the loo.

The more we tried to shift it
The more it stuck like glue
Glaring back with one big eye
The alien down the loo.

It started to get bigger
It grew and grew and grew
Waved its creepy feelers
The alien down the loo.

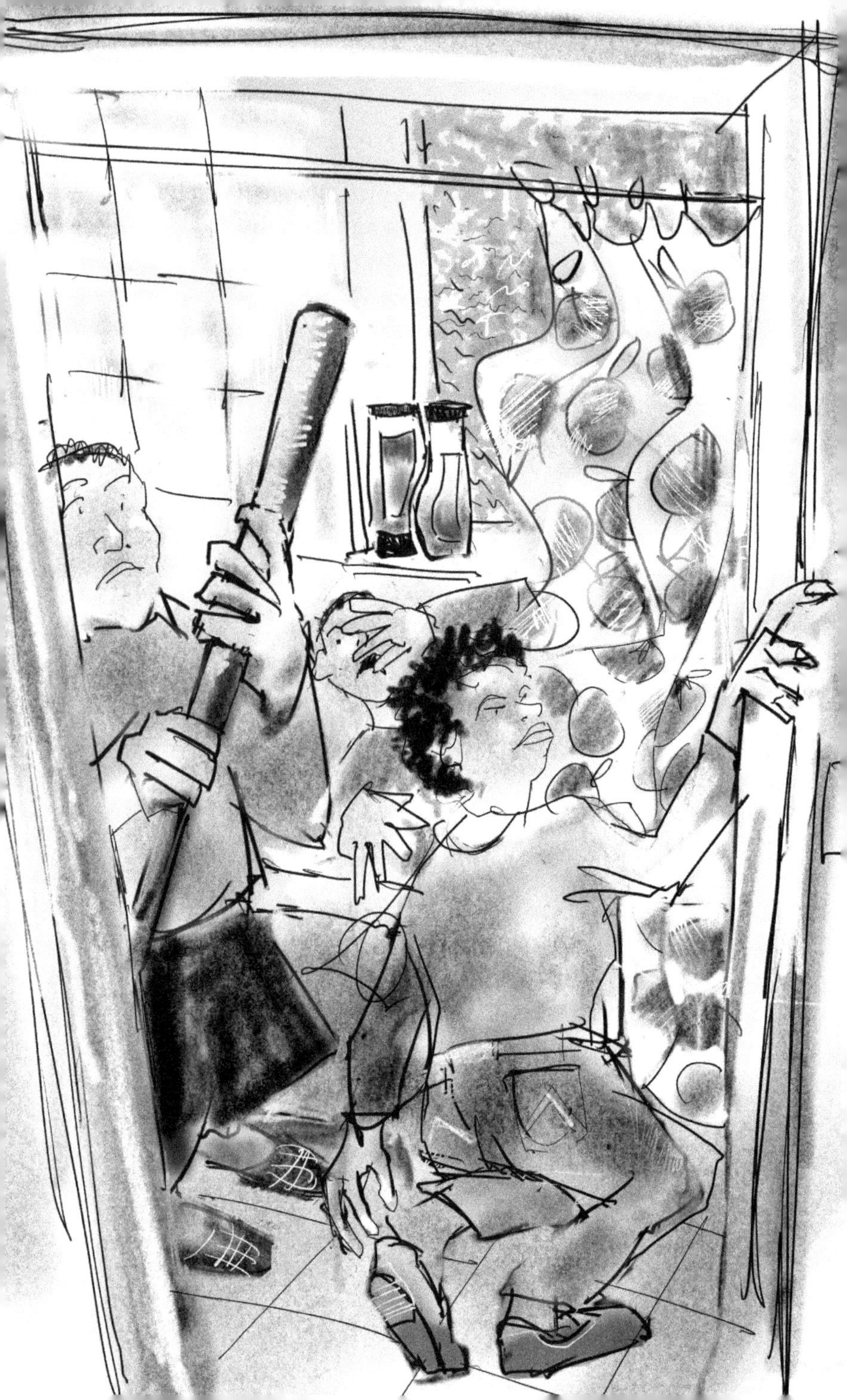

Dad crept up behind it
With his snooker cue
But out it clambered angrily
The alien down the loo.

It sprouted slimy wings
And round the room it flew
We hid inside the shower from
The alien down the loo.

Just then my mum arrived
To mount a brave rescue.
'Just go away,' she yelled at
The alien down the loo.

It tried to bite her head off
She hit it with her shoe
We saw it flap and then collapse
The alien down the loo.

Since then we've never seen it
But if I were you
I'd go and check you haven't got
An alien down the loo.

A VERY TIRED POEM

z z z z z z z z
        zzzzzzzzzz
                zzzzzzzzzzzz zzz zz z
                        b e d
                    a comfy
                    and it will need
                    BREATH
                out of
                extremely
           be
           it will
        PUFF
        PANT
        GASP
      stairs
      p
      e
      e
      t
      s
      y
      r
      e
      v
      these
     climbed
    has
   this poem
  the time
By

T

F

I

L

the
take
just
should
this poem
maybe
or

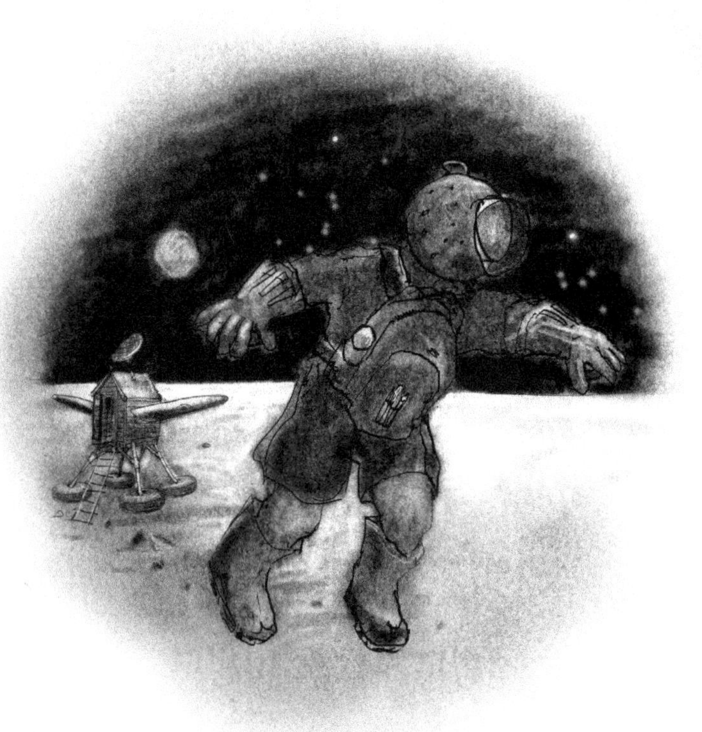

ABOUT DAVID HARMER

David Harmer is best known as a children's writer. He began working in primary schools in 1973. For quite a while he was a class teacher and then a headteacher but he spent many happy years visiting schools, festivals, universities, front rooms and theatres all over the country, working with children and grown-ups too. Sometimes he was with his friend Paul Cookson in their popular performance duo *Spill The Beans*. During this time he has published ten poetry collections and his work has appeared in over 130 anthologies for children.

ABOUT TED SCHOFIELD

Ted started drawing as a boy by copying cartoons. Later, he learned to draw and paint things he could see in the world around him. Ted still paints pictures on canvas but he loves drawing from imagination, often inspired by something funny, and usually on an iPad.

After completing a degree in Fine Art he became an art teacher and then took another degree, this time in illustration. He loves playing the cello, singing in a choir, reading and talking about books, cooking (and eating even more).

ACKNOWLEDGEMENTS

'All Kinds of Kids' and 'Pass It On It's Really True' were first published in *There's A Monster In The Garden* by David Harmer (Frances Lincoln, 2015).

'Grandpa's Stories' was first published in *The Best Ever Book of Funny Poems*, ed. Brian Moses (Macmillans Children's Books, 2021).

'Pasting Patsy's Pasty Posters' and 'Slick Nick's Dog's Tricks' were first published in *The Very Best of David Harmer* (Macmillans Children's Books, 2001).

'My Mum's Put Me On The Transfer List' was first published in *Elephant Dreams* (Macmillan's Children's Books, 1998).

'Daytime Moon' and 'A Goodnight Moon' were first published in *Moonstruck,* ed. Roger Stevens (Otter Barry Books, 2019).

'The History of Nothing' was first published in *Spaced Out*, eds. Brian Moses and James Carter (Bloomsbury, 2019).

'The Visitor', 'Don't Muck About With Giants' and 'Whisper Outside The Graveyard' were first published in *It's Behind You!*, eds. Harmer & Cookson (Macmillans Children's Books, 2010).

'Harry Hobgoblin's Superstore' was first published in *Magic Poems*, ed. John Foster (Oxford University Press, 1997).

An earlier version of 'Pirate Shanty' was first published in *Pirate Poems* by David Harmer (Macmillans Children's Books, 2007).

'Our Tree' was first published in *Earthways Earthwise*, ed. Judith Nicholls (Oxford University Press, 1993).

'One Moment in Summer' and 'Playing Tennis With Justin' were first published in *The Works 3*, ed. Paul Cookson (Macmillans Children's Books, 2004).

'The DIY Astronaut', 'The Worst Place To Find An Alien' and 'Three Happy Birthdays on Faraway Planets' were first published in *It Came From Outer Space* by David Harmer & Paul Cookson (Macmillans Children's Books, 2013).

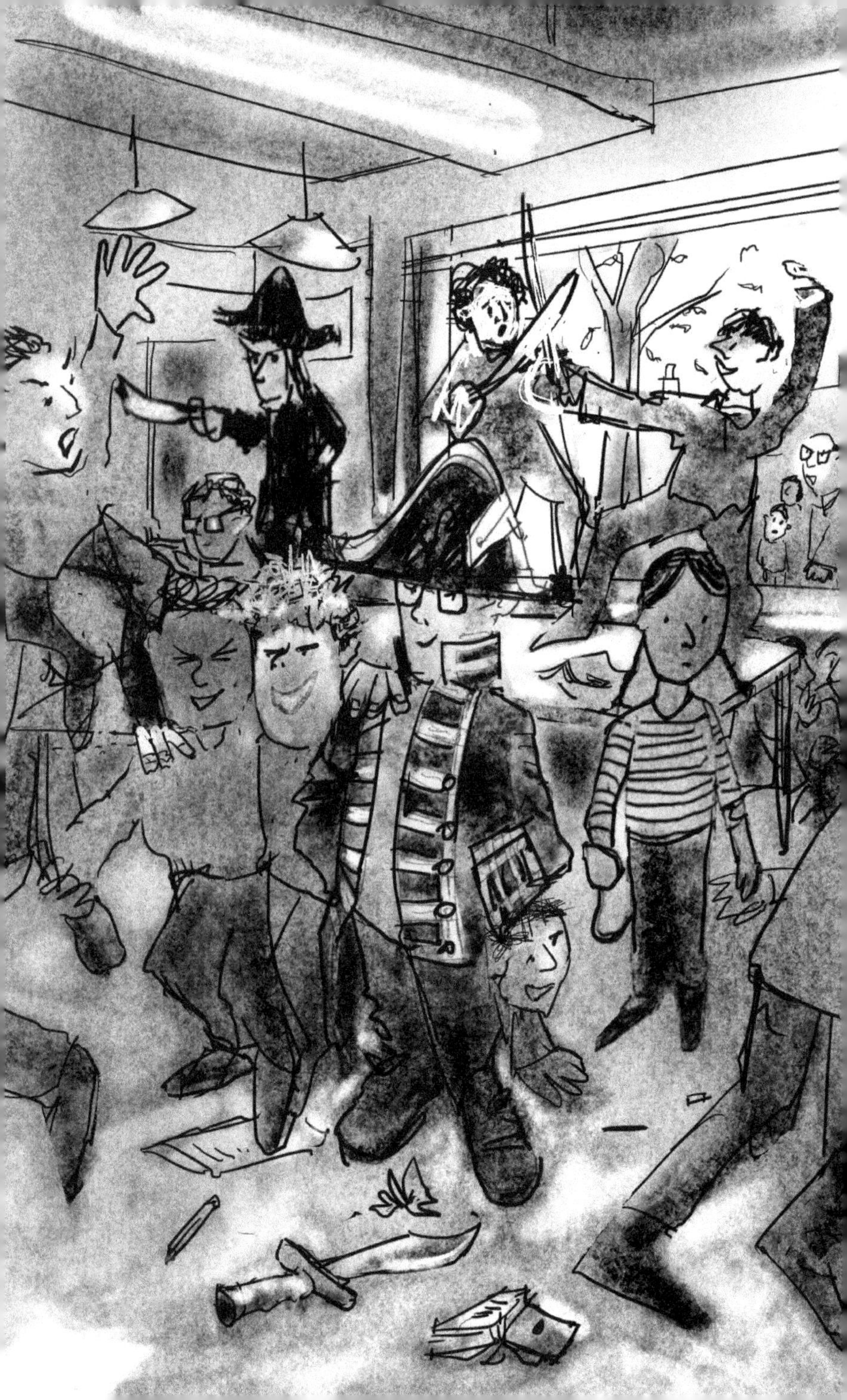